Gypsies of

remembering bygone days

by G.E. C. Webb

with Derek Grant

Published by MD Jones Books
mdjones303@outlook.com

original illustrations by the author

Also by G.E.C. Webb

Gypsies the Secret People

Tom Hathaway

Sinfi's Secret – a Gypsy Family Saga

Gypsies of Dorset
remembering bygone days

Contents

CHAPTER ONE – BEGINNINGS

In my school days in Dorset, way back in the 1920s, I heard tell of a place with an intriguing name; it was called Heavenly Bottom, halfway between Bournemouth and Poole.

"Down Albert Road is Heavenly Bottom", a boy at school told me. "Shouldn't go there; not Heavenly Bottom." But with a name of such romantic sound, how could I not?

Albert Road switch-backed away from the main Ashley Road at a right angle, heading ever downwards. It was lined with houses of weathered red brick, which looked old even then. At the very bottom of the hill, beyond the last house, a rough track turned off to the right;

and there, at the valley floor, a breath-taking sight met my gaze.

So, this was Heavenly Bottom!

I had seen gypsies on the road before but this, it seemed, was their home ground.

Dark-visaged people moved about or sat in groups among various tents and caravans. Horses were tethered nearby, and big, black pots hung from slanting kettle-irons over the glowing wood fires.

A little stream, tributary to Bournemouth's River Bourne as I discovered later, flowed past the site, no doubt supplying the inhabitants with water. Caravans ranged from quite modest small ones to very grand vehicles, with high wheels and elaborate carvings, all picked out in barbaric splendour of colour; red, green, blue, yellow.

There was much polished brass in evidence too. And the tents!

I was fascinated by one big one, a dome-shaped construction, with two arched corridors leading off, one each side. From the very top a thin haze of smoke drifted lazily skyward.

I believe that I sensed at once that these were no ordinary folk who had adopted this way of life. And, indeed, the true Romani, with his raggle-taggle dignity sees himself as the aristocrat, where there are only two sorts of people; Romanis and (all others lumped together) Gorgios. Strongly imbued good manners prevented me from standing and staring. I was fearful of an encounter anyway.

I dawdled by Heavenly Bottom on a number of occasions and I began to wish that I could meet and talk with some of the strange inhabitants.

I was warned that gypsies steal children, but I wasn't particularly worried by that, for there always seemed to be plenty of children there already. Then, one day, a man seated by one of the fires suddenly stood up and called something to me. I didn't catch what he said, but I expect it was some perfectly harmless remark. However, I took fright and made off as fast as I could!

Time passed, and on a number of occasions I saw gypsies on the road, their wagons rumbling along, the men striding purposefully at the horses' heads; always coming from nowhere, heading for nowhere, always as mysterious as when I had first seen them as a boy.

It was some years before I discovered the books of Victorian author George Borrow. His book title "Romano Lavalil" translates to "Gypsy Wordbook". I was delighted to find a glossary of Romani words at the end. I studied it eagerly and committed it to memory. Other books followed, and I increased my vocabulary to fairly respectable proportions. But as yet I had heard no words of Romani spoken. If I approached the gypsy wagons and attempted to talk the gypsy language, could I be sure that my pronunciation would be acceptable to the gypsy ear?

Then, one day in an old green lane, deep in rural Dorset (on the Isle of Purbeck) I had my chance. The lane wound gradually uphill, between bramble hedges and grassy banks, and as I neared the top the scent of wood-smoke assailed my nostrils. This was it!

I knew there were gypsies just a little way ahead. Of course, it could have been any sort of fire – just to burn rubbish, for instance – but I didn't think of that. There were gypsies camped just ahead, of that I felt certain. I walked on the grassy edge so that I could approach them noiselessly. I remember thinking that it would create a better impression to walk silently, as one of them, than to scrunch noisily over the gravel.

I walked slowly, for now that the much longed-for meeting was at hand, I was shy of trying my meagre knowledge of Romani on a party of seasoned travellers who had used it every day from birth. But as I topped the rise, I saw that there was only one wagon.

You mustn't call it a caravan, by the way. In English, it is a wagon; the Romani word is vardo. A man was sprawled on his back, full-length before the fire, his battered hat over his eyes, and a woman with a small child on her knee sat on the steps of the wagon. Three other children were playing near at hand, and a lurcher dog pricked up his ears as I approached.

I walked on towards the little group, raised my right hand, and said, "Sar shan?" wondering if I was pronouncing the words correctly.

The result was disappointing, for no Romani words were given in exchange. "Afternoon", the man replied, watching me closely. He was summing me up. No doubt he had met plenty of gorgies before and, at first, he probably suspected that I was coming to move him on. But here was no veshengro (no gamekeeper), wanting to turn him away from his good camping place in the green lane; here was a rather unusual specimen of gorgio.

For whoever heard of a gorgio coming up to a Romanichal and greeting him in words of the old language. He was at a loss to understand what it was all about. I was at a loss too, but I persevered.

They were a young couple; the man no man than about twenty-five and the woman perhaps twenty-three. The man wore the usual shapeless felt hat and drab-coloured suit, a trifle ragged here and there, big hob-nailed boots and, of course, a coloured neckerchief. The woman wore a red and yellow patterned headscarf (the bori diklo, as they call it), beneath which was displayed a wealth of hair; black, shining and coarse, like a horse's tale. She had the black, pointed oriental eyes of the Romani race.

Neither she nor her husband, nor indeed the children, took their eyes from my face. They all watched me distrustfully as I plodded on, drawing on my meagre knowledge of Romani.

Still I heard no Romani words in reply. I produced some cigarettes (I was a smoker in those days). "Toovalo?" I said; "Tobacco?" The woman took one and placed it between her lips. The man took one, deftly slit it with a thumbnail and stuffed the tobacco into a clay pipe.

I could think of nothing else to say. How did old Borrow, Sampson, Leyland and the rest get in touch with the secret people? Here was I, actually in the camp of this young couple, speaking words of their own tongue to them, and them being frigidly polite to me, answering only in English. Then the woman, with gypsy intuition, evidently summed me up as harmless. "Do you write books?" she fired at me.

"Yes", I admitted, that was it; I was a writer.

Suddenly the man barked at me, "What's a pookerin' kosh?" And I knew the answer to that one. I said. That, I had read was the question that gypsies usually asked of Gorgios that claimed to know their speech. And here was I, sitting beside a gypsy fire in the wilds of rural Dorset, being asked "What's a pookerin' kosh?"

Here was a member of the mysterious Romani race, a speaker of the pogado jib from early childhood, smiling at me through the smoke of a wood fire and asking me "What's a pookerin' kosh?"

"It's a signpost", I said, triumphantly. "It's a speaking stick that tells the road".

"Quite the Romani rai, ain't you?" said the woman.

I saw that her rather severe expression had relaxed, and she was smiling too. The word "rai" really means gentleman, but if a gypsy calls you a Romani rai he doesn't mean exactly that. He means that although you are a gorgio, an outsider, you're not really such a bad sort of fellow because although you live in a house and are not of his race, you know something of the travelling people and can be accepted as a friend. I was probably a half-wit; who else would write words in a book?

But I was harmless and would be good company for an hour or so. And so, I spent a happy hour in the company of the gypsy couple and their family. It amused them to ask me if I knew the Romani words for all sorts of things.

Some I knew and some they told me, and from time to time they laughed uproariously when I mispronounced a word. Altogether I felt highly delighted with my encounter. Could I come and see them again tomorrow? "Yes, certainly come tomorrow". There would be a cup of meski (a cup of tea) and we could exchange words of the old language again beside the fire.

Their "goodnight and good luck" in Romani rang in my ears as I walked back down the lane. I would certainly come and visit the gypsy family tomorrow, I decided, and I would bring my camera with me and get a few pictures.

Accordingly, I set off full of hope the following afternoon. I topped the rise, where I had seen the gypsies the previous day, but they were gone!

There was the blackened ring on the ground where the fire had been, where we had sat yesterday and talked Romani. There were the wheel tracks of the wagon and the imprint of the horses' hooves; nothing more. As for the blackened ring on the ground, I was to know it often in times to come.

The Romani language has greatly declined, and it survives only as the pagado jib, the broken tongue. Sentences are constructed in English, but a Romani word is substituted and inserted here and there, so that it is unintelligible to anyone who doesn't jin the poker (understand the speech). When they first appeared in this country, several centuries ago, they were dubbed gypsies because of the belief that they had come from Egypt.

From the fifteenth century onwards, various records refer to them as "the lords of little Egypt" and similar fanciful titles. But, although Egypt seems to have been one of the countries through which they wandered, Egypt was not their starting place. It was India from whence they came in the first place. The clue is in the Romani language, which bears a close resemblance to dialects in use in that country to this day by people who live in the same nomadic way as our British gypsies.

One morning, a couple of years after the end of the last war, I saw a gypsy wagon pulled in the rough grass, bordering a little-used road near Wimborne. It was a small wagon, though obviously well-kept, although it was basically simple in design. There were green and white curtains at the windows and a lot of carving along the wooden sides.

A man with a cap on the back of his head and a yellow neckerchief knotted about his throat was standing precariously on a pile of logs and old boxes. He was busily painting his wagon. By now I had become more wily and knew better than to force myself upon him too quickly.

He was painting his wagon and, as far as I could judge, that meant that he would remain where he was for several days and I should be able to make his acquaintance gradually. And so I walked on, without reducing my pace. When I was opposite him and no more than twenty yards away, I raised my right hand in the approved fashion and greeted him, "Sar shan?"

He looked round, rapidly raised his right hand with the paint brush in it, and as quickly returned to his painting. He said not a word, but he had acknowledged my greeting in the gypsy way.

I knew better than to force the pace, and I walked on without a backward glance as though I was completely disinterested. He little knew what an interest he had really aroused, or perhaps he did for the Romanichals have an uncanny insight into human nature and often seem to know a great deal about what is going on inside the head of a gorgio.

I passed the wagon again in the evening and the man had finished the roof in a pale green colour. He had also done the back end and most of one side in royal blue and now he was standing back, brush in hand, his wife by his side, admiring his handiwork. Again, I walked past without stopping, but this time I called out in Romani, "Been a nice day, man".

"Yes", he replied. Then, with one of those wide, graceful movements which are characteristic of the race, he swept his hand round and up towards the late afternoon sky.

"Bavol will be up torarti", he said. And he turned back abruptly in contemplation of his wagon. Bavol will be up torarti, he had said. The wind will be up tonight. It was frightfully corrupted and mixed Romani, and it might well have caused the man's grandfather to turn in his grave.

Later I was to hear more of this grandfather, but more of that in its proper place. Yes, it was frightfully corrupted Romani, but nevertheless a fair example of gypsy speech today. And, of course, it matters not for it is secret enough for the veshengros and the gavers (the gamekeepers and the policemen).

But to return to the man who was painting his wagon.

I passed his camp again on the following morning to find him harnessing a shaggy little pony to a light cart, preparatory to setting off on some unknown business of his own. When I passed again in the evening, I saw that he had finished all the royal blue paint work on the body of his wagon and had started to pick out the window frames in chrome yellow.

But now, it seemed, he had finished painting for the day, for he was lounging on the bank beside the road, whittling a stick and smoking. This time I stopped and admired his handiwork.

"Nice vardo that", I said, nodding towards the wagon. Now that I was close to him, I saw that he was quite a young man and I put his age at being round about the middle twenties. He made no comment in reply to my remark, but I think he took it to be sincere, as indeed it was.

He stood there beside the road regarding me with a half-startled look, like that of a wild animal, with his slanting black eyes. But I suppose he summed me up as harmless, for we soon got down to a discussion on painting. I made suitably polite remarks about the part he had already done and admired the yellow window frames against the royal blue body. I asked him what colour he was going to paint the wheels.

"I always paints the wheels red", he explained. "And I always paints yeller lines down the spokes. But", he added reflectively, "You ought to have seen my old Granddad, how he would paint up a wagon. I remember when I was a little chavo, about eight or nine I would have been.

"We was stopping with the old 'uns, down in Dorset I think it was. We must have been there three or four weeks. And my old Granddad, he painted up his wagon while we was there. Beautiful it was to see him. Us little 'uns, we'd stand and watch him for hours.

"All the colours he used. Well, I reckon there was hundreds of 'em; well, about twenty anyway. All different reds and greens and blues and yellers; you never seen nothing like it. And he done all little carved bits all round; all dear little birds and all leaves and fruit an' that, all painted just like real – beautiful. Just about all the colours there was my old Granddad would use. Well, all except one. 'Course, he was a proper old-fashioned Romani, talked the old language like anything, he could. Proper deep Romani it was he could speak. There none left like him on the road today."

"And what was the colour he wouldn't have on his vardo?" I asked the man, bringing him up with a jerk.

He looked at me solemnly and said, "Black".

Just the one word … black.

After a pause he went on. "You don't never have to put no black on a wagon", the old man would say. "You paint black on a wagon and somebody in the family will be dead before the new moon", he'd say.

"Well, of course," I said, "I suppose that's right. People wear black clothes for funerals and funeral trappings are black."

"No, no, that ain't the same," the gypsy man said. "You can wear black clothes an' black trousers an' black 'ats an' that, and it don't do no 'arm, see. But you don't have to put no black on the wagon."

"What about your own wagon? The stovepipe, for instance. Won't you put a bit of black on that?"

"Now see, rai, I wouldn't put no black on my wagon; not for anything, I wouldn't. Though I knows a few travellers now what don't mind about that. But that's because they're only 'alf-breed didakais. Can't say as I know any tatcho Romanichals, any true Romanichals, as would do that. No, I shall paint my stovepipe with aluminium. Don't last all that long, not with rain and gettin' 'ot an' all that, but not black I wouldn't never 'ave.

While he had been talking, the man's wife had stood silently inside the wagon, regarding us over the half-door.

I thought she was looking rather disapproving, to see her husband conversing at such length with an unknown gorgio. But perhaps I was wrong, for when I looked back when I was some distance down the road, the two were seated by the fire and were taking no further notice of me.

I eventually got to know this man quite well, but not on the morrow for when I returned, once again they had gone!

There was the blackened ring, with which by now I was familiar. That was all.

CHAPTER TWO - DISCOVERIES

It must have been a year later that I again met Dewie Cooper, as I found he was called. It was in the same place where I had first seen him painting his vardo. This time there was another wagon pulled in, a little way away from his own, housing, I was told, "My missus' auntie".

I was given to understand that the unfortunate husband of the aunt, owing to some misunderstanding about a pheasant, had been "lullered by the gavers and sent by the bitcherin'-moosh to stiraben". That is to say, taken by the police and sent by the magistrates to prison; a state of affairs that, unhappily, is not altogether unknown in little Egypt.

Meanwhile the aunt was travelling with Dewie and his wife. She didn't appear to want to have any dealings with me; no doubt she had seen enough of Gorgios for the time being.

Dewie, on the other hand, seemed not displeased to while away an hour in my company while his wife was "over there with her Auntie, talking enough to talk the hind leg off a donkey," as he put it. His wagon, now that it was finished, certainly looked a fine vehicle. The carved strip running right round the body and picked out in red, yellow, and green set if off to a nicety.

"I'd have thought your old Granddad would have thought it a good job", I said.

Dewie laughed. "No, t'wouldn't have done for the old moosh; not enough colours."

"I suppose the old man is dead now?" I asked.

"Yes", replied Dewie, "He died a good few years back. Proper big funeral we 'ad for the old moosh. Why, you wouldn't never see a gorgio coffin anything like it. See, they had to have it big 'cause the old moosh was a real kushti boshomengro."

He paused and sat looking reflectively into the fire.

I was considerably surprised to hear that a large coffin was necessary, because the old man was a kushti boshomengro (a fine violinist). "And why is a big coffin necessary for a kushti boshomengro?" I ventured.

"Ah! Well, it ain't, not for every boshomengro. But the old man, he was that fond of his old fiddle that he never wanted it to be broken up when he died. 'When I'm gone', he says, 'When I'm gone, you lay the old fiddle in the coffin 'long with me.' 'Cause you knows, rai, our people always burns all the things what belongs to anyone who dies, or else they breaks them up. And if they don't do that then the different things what's left has to go in the coffin 'long with 'em."

I was fascinated, and wanted to learn more.

"Yes," Dewie went on, with obvious pride for the doings of his family, "Yes, there was Romanichals come from all over to walk behind the old man's coffin. And, before the funeral, there was wagons coming and stopping there, where we was stopped at the time, and all the people filing into his wagon where he was lyin'. And they had his little oil lamp hung up and kept alight all the time. And all the time, day and night, before the funeral, there was always somebody sitting up with him.

"Course, nobody went to bed while they was waiting for the funeral, not none of the grown-up ones, you understands, rai. I well remembers my Dad said, 'Now, Dewie, you're old enough to do like the men do now. So, there's no bed for you 'til the funeral's over,' he says. 'Course, I was mighty proud to be doin' like the men. There was always three of 'em sat with the old while 'e was lyin' there in 'is wagon. 'Cause for why? Well, supposing there was only two; well, one of 'em might doze off and leave the other one alone with the ghost. So, you see, there 'as to be three. And in all the three days we was there we never ate nothing; not no proper meat or nothin' like that, just a bit of bread and some water to drink.

"All the time there was more wagons kept coming and stopping, 'til at last a couple of policemen comes a-ridin' on bicycles and says as 'ow we 'ave to move off. But, as luck would 'ave it, who should be coming down the road but the tompad; yes, the parson, just as them two policemens got there. 'Now what are you doin', old friends?' the parson says to the policemen.

'Well, sir,' they says, 'We 'ave to move these 'ere people on. 'Tis orders,' they says. Then that old parson, he says, 'But these people aren't doin' no 'arm. And, what's more, do you know as 'ow you are in the presence of death?' he says.

"Then the policemen says no, they didn't know nothing about that; only that they had to move us on. But that parson, 'e was a decent old moosh and 'e got them policemen to go away. 'You needn't worry about 'avin' to move', 'e says, 'not until after the funeral. And we didn't see them policemen again, though we all moved out after the funeral and we was all off afore the sun was up next mornin'.'"

Mesmerised, I could only sit and listen as the amazing tale unfolded further.

"Well, I've told you was such a big coffin we had for the old man. In there with 'im was 'is old fiddle, what he thought such a lot of. And 'e was wearing 'is new suit what he'd only had on a time or two. An' they put 'is whip in 'is 'and 'is old tobaccy jar with the squirrel on the lid (his tail being the 'andle to pick it up with, see). Oh, and a lot of other things, but I disremember them now.

"Well, at last they sets off. Now my mother, she says to all of us young 'uns to be very careful how we went. For, she says, to stumble while following someone in a coffin is to make your own grave ready before the year's out. Four of the blackest horses you ever did see was pullin' the hearse. Then there was three carriages for the older people.

"After that, all the other Romanichals followed, walkin' four lines wide all along the road; well, hundreds there must have been. It looked like a great snake to see them coming all down over the hill. Then, when we gets to the gates of the churchyard, there was the old parson with 'is white 'air and dressed all in 'is long white shirt, standing there a-waitin' for us. We didn't 'ave no service in the church, like the gorgies does, for my Uncle Benjie (him bein' the old moosh's oldest son), 'e says to the parson, 'No', 'e says, 'The old man wouldn't want to be took inside. Let 'im 'ave the blessed word said over 'im out in the sunshine by the grave; 'im what's never been in a kenner all 'is jivaben'.

"Only, a-course, not the Romani words 'e didn't say; 'What's never been in a house all his life', 'e says. And so the parson, he led the way to the grave what 'ad been dug just by the hedge by the end of the churchyard. Then 'e reads out the blessed words from 'is book what 'e 'ad in 'is 'and."

"When they had lowered the coffin down into the grave", Dewi went on, "all the Romanichals walked slowly passed, and everyone looks down at the coffin for the last time. One or two of 'em, they drops in a penny or two. And Uncle Benji, 'e takes a bottle of beer out of 'is pocket and, taking out the stopper, 'e pours a drop into the grave; 'just a drop for the journey, me old Dad', 'e says.

"And all the time nobody made a sound, 'cept when one or other of them would bend over the grave and say a word or two of farewell to the old man. But everyone was behaved most proper; it was beautiful to see. Of course, there were no tears; for, you know sir, tears is a disturbance for the dead."

"Well, when it was all over, we all goes back to the stopping-place. They all stands round in a great big ring while Uncle Benji, he gets out his knife and 'e cuts the old man's harness all to bits. Then 'e batters 'is brasses all one by one with a big stone. Then 'e gets up into the wagon with a great bundle of straw, which 'e breaks open and spreads about inside. And 'e takes all the bits of 'arness and piles them up in the middle of the floor. Then 'e rips up the old man's bed and 'e piles that up.

"And then he goes and 'e pulls a burning branch out of the fire and 'e flings it through the doorway. There was a lot of smoke at first, 'til Uncle Benji, 'e ups with a big stone and 'e flings it through one o' the winduhs. That seemed to let a draught through, or sommink. The flames soon burned up bright, through the winduhs and right out through the roof. Ah, a good vardo that was.

"Soon it was all burned away, and then Uncle Benji and some of the other men, they takes 'is spoon and fork and 'is knife and 'is cup and 'is plate, and they batters them all up with the old man's kettle iron. And they digs a big 'ole there, by the ashes of 'is wagon and buries 'em all, the kettle iron with 'em, so nobody shouldn't ever use 'em again. Then there was the old man's three 'orses; off they was sent to the knackers and killed.

"And when it was all done, the women gets out clean white cloths on the ground and they brings out all the food, see. For by now we was mighty 'ungry. And there was such a hawin' and a peevin'; such an eatin' and a drinkin'. Then we all goes to sleep, but we was up before the sun in the mornin' and all gone our different ways."

Well could I imagine the busy scene after the funeral; and the feast, and the almost magical disappearance of the whole party before sun-up the next morning.

There again would have been the blackened rings on the ground. Dewi was undoubtedly exaggerating when he said that hundreds of Romanichals followed his grandfather's coffin. He was carried away, as gypsies often are, by his own eloquence.

Nevertheless, large numbers of gypsies do attend the funerals of their people. A resident of Woodgreen, just north of Wimborne on the way to Witchampton, told me that she witnessed a gypsy funeral there. It must have been a funeral in a very poor family, for she said that the coffin was wheeled on a handcart. But a vast concourse of people followed it, she told me.

And I was reminded of Dewi's words when she used his own simile. "A great crowd of gypsies followed the coffin", she said. "When I first saw the procession in the distance, it looked like a great snake winding along the road."

I would think that Dewi Cooper's account of his grandfather's funeral was a fairly good record of gypsy ways in such matters. But today such wholesale destruction doesn't seem to be carried out. I have heard of gypsy funerals where the corpse was laid out in a tent, especially erected for the purpose. After the funeral, this tent was burned, instead of the wagon. But the total destruction of everything, including some very fine living-wagons, has undoubtedly taken place in the past.

There is another, lesser known, custom connected with death that is practised in some families. When a member of these families dies, as a result of an accident, a cross of pebbles is laid out near the spot and trampled level with the surrounding earth.

The Romanichals, as might be expected in an oriental race, have great respect for the dead; and I have heard of several instances where bereaved gypsies have made an annual pilgrimage to a grave for many years. Death by accident, falls from wagons and carting mishaps are all too common among the tents and wagons.

There has been a gypsy settlement at Woodgreen for many years. The villagers there tell several versions of a sad little story of the young wife of Bob Cooper. I think the story, as told to me about forty years ago by her niece, who said she was an eyewitness, is pretty accurate.

"I was only a little girl at the time", she began, "but I remember it was bank holiday. It might have been Easter, it might have been Whitsun, I disremembers. They'd been down to the village, to the kitchema; the pub, you understands, sir. We was just stoppin' by them woods you can see up there. They 'ad a little cart and a pony.

"Uncle Bob, 'e reins up the pony and 'e gets down from the cart. And then, dordi! Dordi! Terrible it is to tell! Poor, dear Auntie was just a-steppin' back, down out of the little cart when, nobody knows for why, the horsie suddenly moved off. And my auntie, she falls right down on the ground on 'er poor 'ead. My poor Uncle Bob, struck nearly crazy 'e was, and all the other men and women come a-runnin' up to see what 'appened. There weren't nothin' they could do; 'er neck was broke. And the drabengro when 'e comes, the doctor, 'e just shakes 'is 'ead 'cause there wasn't nothing they could do."

The gypsy woman was obviously deeply moved to be recounting this story, although the event happened forty years before. After a pause, she went on, "Poor Uncle Bob, proper broke him up it did. And they couldn't get 'im to move from the place where it 'appened. And I dare say you've seen 'ow our people makes a cross of stones. Well, 'e got a lot of stones together and 'e made a cross of stones, just by where it 'appened. There on the bank, just by where she died.

"And every year when the day come round when his missus died, 'e come back to the place and 'e put back any of the stones what might 'ave got moved, so as to make the cross again. And he'd pick out all bits of grass an' weeds an'that. I've been there with the poor old man many a time. It was only a few years back he died hisself, but 'e never got over it. And the stone cross, 'e always kept fresh as the day 'e made it."

Such was the story of this tragedy among the tents and wagons of the Stour Valley.

The woman's husband walked along with me, to show me the spot where Bob Cooper, in his despair, had made his cross of stones; his pathetic little monument to his wife's memory. "It's just along by that there thorn bush", he said, pointing. But when we reached the bush, it was difficult to make anything of the few stones remaining in place, half-hidden as they were in the long grass.

The thorn bush seemed to me to be appropriate. Many gypsy graves, in many country churchyards, have had thorn bushes planted on them. Could it be connected with memories of burials in unconsecrated ground?

Many such burials must have taken place in the past. Or could it be a survival of some very ancient Romani custom, dating back through the centuries when wayside burials were made in some eastern land? Then a thorn bush and a heap of stones would have been a natural barrier to prevent wild beasts from molesting the grave. We shall never know.

When somebody dies, the name of the deceased is not spoken, in case it should call up the ghost. After the passage of time the rule is relaxed. But I noticed that, even after the lapse of so many years, the name of the auntie was not given.

I think that it may have been because of the very tragic circumstances that the niece referred only to "my poor Auntie" – nameless. It is not surprising that the gypsy has many superstitions, living as he does; cheek to cheek with mother earth, right at nature's heart. It would be much more surprising if he were without superstition.

Things that seem quite ridiculous under the electric light, between solid walls, take on an entirely different significance under the stars on Cranborne heath, and in the black night on the woodland.

He is not without religious beliefs too. I remember old Nelson, one fine spring morning, squatting by the roadside, smoking his old black pipe. I had met Lavendi and Nelson, and their several daughters and sons-in-law, who usually travelled with them, on previous occasions. The old man greeted me, as also did two of the sons-in-law who were with him. We talked for a while and then I asked Nelson if I might take his photograph. He was quite a character! He reckoned he was "more than eighty a goodish bit", and with his weather-beaten face, black felt hat and hobnail boots, he looked one of the best camera studies I had ever seen.

He was wearing a pair of old-fashioned spectacles that morning. I discovered afterwards that he had picked them up on the road many years before and regarded them as a lucky possession.

He wore them often when he was resting, but I noticed that he always took them off to look at anything; I imagine that they were quit unsuitable for his eyes and he found them a considerable handicap. But this morning he was sitting by the roadside smoking and, as he had nothing in particular to do, he was wearing his spectacles. He could always look over the top of them, at a pinch, anyway.

When I suggested taking his photograph, he began to hedge. I expected that he was afraid that his likeness would appear in some newspaper. Most gypsies enjoy having their photograph taken, if they can be sure of receiving a copy afterwards, but many of them don't like the idea of their photographs appearing in gorgio newspapers.

I began reassuring him that I had no intention of using his photograph in a newspaper. But one of his sons-in-law broke in, "No, it ain't that, rai; you can take our photos if you like", and he indicated the other man with him. "But the old moosh, 'e won't have 'is photo took on account of it's Sunday."

Of course, I told Nelson that I respected his wishes in the matter and I would say no more about taking his photograph. At that he told me, "All my life I ain't never even chinned a kosh on a Sundee (never even cut a stick on a Sundee). And I always reckons never to move from the place where we're stoppin', never to 'arness up a horse on a Sundee; well, not unless I've 'ad to on account of the police movin' us on. Don't take no notice of a Sundee, the policemen don't."

I met a strong dislike of my camera on another occasion, although for a different reason.

I was with my old friends the Boswells; voluble Leda and Piramus, who were tacitor and spouse – and often to be found (for a short while each time) near or around Wareham, Wool or

Moreton. Would they like me to take their photograph, I suggested, so that they could keep a copy of it in their wagon and bring it out to show their people on occasion. Leda threw up her hands and wailed, "Dordi! Dordi!"

I must have looked rather astonished.

Piramus said, "I don't mind". Then he jerked his head in the direction of his wife. "Thinks it will spoil her fortune-tellin'", he added. He proceeded to fill his pipe, ramming down the tobacco slowly with a firm finger. I could see that he would say no more.

Leda, on this occasion, seemed strangely at a loss for words. "I've always got on all right with the dukkerin', the fortunes an' that", she said after a while. "Many fortunes I've told at the houses of the gorgio women. And mind you, rai, a good many of them would tell you that things have worked out just like I told them they would." She sat herself more upright as she got into her stride again. I don't think there is anything on earth that could stop Leda talking for any length of time.

"Yes, a good bit of true fortune-tellin' I can do", she went on. "Oh yes, a good bit of the truest of the true tatcho dukkerin'.

"One day the wife of that young gent, now," and Leda named the young woman and the village where she lived. "Yes, a pretty young gal she was. Worried about 'er 'usband, she was. Only a young chap 'e was, and seemed 'e was a soldier. Well, an officer 'e was, really, and 'e was in some foreign part somewhere and 'e 'and't been 'eard of for some time. And she was beginnin' to think as 'ow 'e wouldn't never come back no more.

"But when she talked to me about it, it seemed to me I could see the young man, clear as could be; looked that hot, 'e did, just short trousers and an open shirt 'e 'ad on, and 'is boots o' course. But real sweatin' with the 'otness 'e was. So, I says to 'er, I says, 'Would it be very 'ot where 'e is, me young lady?' 'Oh yes', she says, 'It's a very 'ot country where 'e 'is'. 'Well', I says to 'er, 'I sees 'im plain as can be, walkin' along sweating because it's so 'ot.

"And the other soldiers, they're all followin' along with 'im. There's two or three got a job to get along; they looks as though they been 'urt,' I says. 'And there's one being carried on something, four soldier men there is a-carryin' of 'im. Yes, there's some of 'em been 'urt cruel bad. But not your man,' I says, 'strong an' 'andsome, 'e is, and 'e's walkin' along in front showing the others where to go.

"And soon they'll come to the end of their journey, out of the thick woods where they're strugglin' along now,' I says. 'Soon they'll be back with their friends, and you'll be 'earing as how 'e's all right and comin' back to you again.' Give me five bob, that young lady did," Leda went on, "two 'alf crowns. 'Cause see, I told 'er what she wanted to know".

Those were her very words.

"Oh yes, rai," Leda added, turning more squarely towards me, "oh yes, I knows what you're thinkin'. I knows there's fortune-tellin' what ain't true, but them things what I told that young rakli was all true. Not only was they what she was wantin' to 'ear, but she knowed I was tellin' the truth."

I didn't doubt that the woman believed the words that Leda had told her.

Anyone meeting Leda for the first time, and hearing her husky voice rising and falling, and held by the penetrating gaze of her black Romani eyes, would be hypnotised into believing almost anything that the gypsy woman desired. And yet, there was often something in what Leda told. Indeed, there was on this occasion, for the young officer did return from the swamps and jungles of wartime Malaysia, just as Leda had foretold.

"Don't ask me 'ow it is, I dunno. But this I do know."

She drew herself up and rose, slowly, to a standing position. "That there camera what you've got ain't goin' to dik at mandi's mooi with his narkri yock". By which I gathered that she wasn't going to have my camera looking at her face with his evil eye.

Leda was quite serious.

The silent Piramus was delighted to appear in the picture and it was only with great difficulty that I managed to persuade him to refrain from sitting bolt upright, in an impossibly rigid position, and staring hard at the narkri yock (the evil eye) that had so unnerved his wife.

Leda did not draw out of range of the camera, still muttering about narkri yock dikking at mandi's mooi. She squatted in the background, covering her face with both hands so that the camera could not see her. But, all the same, taking a lively interest in what was going on, by watching me through the cracks between her fingers.

When it was all over and the camera safely back in its case, Leda visibly relaxed. The moment of danger had passed!

CHAPTER THREE –
MORE DISCLOSURES

The next time I encountered her, I asked Leda more about her dislike of the camera and its evil eye.

"Wouldn't have that evil thing lookin' at me, not for anything, I wouldn't", she said. "I've just been telling you about my dukkerin', about me fortune-tellin'. Real true it is; realest, truest truth, my fortune-tellin' is. If that thing was to look at me and take my likeness, shut up inside that there black box, well, I wouldn't be able to tell true fortunes no more."

"You mean that if your likeness was taken, it would actually take something of yourself away then, Leda?" I asked her.

She nodded vigorously. "Course it would. How could that box 'ave a likeness of somebody in it, without it take something of the man or the woman away from them?" she reasoned. "Must do, don't it?"

I thought this over and then I said, "But you don't mind looking in a mirror, Leda? Aren't you afraid that it may spoil your dukkerin' powers?"

"No", answered the gypsy woman, "oh no, that ain't the same at all. Cause for why, you ask?

"Well, true it is what you says, that you sees your picture in the looking glass; takes your picture, the looking glass do, but it don't take nothin' away from you. See, 'cause you only has to walk away and there you are, back to where you was before you looked in the dicker-glim. It takes your picture, the looking glass do, but it don't keep it; gives it back to you, as soon as you goes away from it, see."

I nodded my head to show that I understood. I was delighted with the whole reasoning. Who, but a gypsy, could think along such lines? And yet Leda was no fool. And she certainly knew more than anyone I had ever met when it came to fortune-telling.

Leda got up and threw a few pieces of wood on the fire. She picked up the big, black iron kettle from its place near at hand. It appeared to be already filled, for she straight away hung it from the kettle iron over the flames.

Four brown and white hens, with a brown cockerel strolling importantly among them, pecked, and scratched around the camp. It always amazed me that they should never stray far from the wagon. When the gypsies were on the road, the chickens remained in a coop, carried beneath the wagon. But as soon as a new camp was made, they were released and spent their time, as now, no further than ten yards or so from the vardo.

"We likes the eggs for breakfast," Leda told me once. "Eggs for breakfast, just like the gorgies does."

I have noticed that some gypsies who keep chickens tether just one bird with a string tied to one leg, just above the foot; the other end of the string being tied to a peg, driven into the ground. But Piramus seemed to manage well enough, without such tethering.

On this occasion, Piramus was not busy polishing his large collection of horse brasses, nor was he cleaning the harness; instead, he was working on an old flat cart that he had recently acquired from goodness know where. It was an uninspiring-looking vehicle, just a flat platform, boarded over.

The rear end was supported by an axle with two iron-shod wheels. Two smaller wheels on a swivelling axle, with shaft attached, supported the front. There was nothing more to the vehicle than that. But the industrious Piramus was determined to make something artistic out of it. All around the narrow, wooden sides he was carving a pattern of diamonds in a sort of bas-relief.

For tools he had no more than on ordinary, domestic table knife, with half the length of its blade broken off, the remaining piece much sharpened. It served both as a gauge for measuring the length of each diamond and as a means of cutting the wood. Each straight side was exactly as wide as the knife-blade.

This type of decoration is typically gypsy; triangles, squares, rectangles, and diamonds. I have seen them on the sides and the ends of vardos, along carts and even along the sides of shafts. Piramus must have spent quite a long time carving the sides of his flat cart – his trolley, as he called it. But when I called on him and Leda on this occasion, it was almost done. In fact, by the time Leda had made the tea, Piramus had only two more diamonds to do.

He took the cup which his wife handed to him and placed it on the end of the trolley beside him, while he finished the job. "Bit hot, I expect," he commented, laconically. In a few minutes, the job was complete and Piramus had made the last cut. He put down the knife beside the cup, stretched and yawned, before taking his tea and sipping it.

"A good job that, me old moosh," commented Leda. "Gonna start paintin' now, are you?" Piramus nodded. He climbed the five steps of the wagon and disappeared inside, reappearing in a moment with a small tin of paint and a little brush. He placed them both on the flat platform of the trolley, while he swallowed the remainder of his tea.

Then he levered off the lid of the tin, picked up a piece of stick from the ground and, after shaving the end clean with his knife, started to stir the paint. Piramus painted every third diamond red. In a very short time, he had finished one side of the trolley and had started on the front end. "Red and yeller and green it's gonna be when it's finished," Leda informed me. "Red and yeller, proper Romani colours they is. I reckon there's more of our people choose red and yeller for anything like that than any other colours at all. You ought to 'ave seen the wagon our Dad had; all the colours you could think of he done that. But what you would notice most of all was the red and the yeller."

Then I remembered what Dewi Cooper had told me once – you must never put black on the wagon. So, I asked Leda about it. "You say that your Dad painted his vardo all the different colours you could think of?" I asked.

"Yes," she replied. "That's right, all the different colours you could think of. That many different colours there was..." She went on to describe the wagon in detail. It was several minutes before I could manage to get a word in again.

"Yes," I said at last, when she paused for breath, "but what about black?"

Leda looked at me in a pitying sort of way. "Black?" she said, incredulously. "Black? On a vardo? No, there ain't no real Romanis as I know that would do that. Least ways, there aren't no true romanichal I knows who would do that. Course, nowadays, with all of them 'alf-bred didakais; well, I suppose some of them wouldn't know no better. But not in them days you wouldn't find it, not with tatcho romanichals anyway.

"Course, theres other things with the posh-rats, the 'alf-breed gypsies I mean, see. I won't say as 'ow some of them ain't all right. But you get a Romani wedded to a gorgio and the children inherits the worst of both of them, I says. No good don't come of it, not as a rule it don't anyway. Now all of us people likes a dog, as you well knows. Take my Piramus now, real fond of that there dog, he is. And a good dog for getting a rabbit now and again, he is."

The dog in question – a lean, long-legged, brindled animal, not far removed from a greyhound – was stretched beneath the cart on which Piramus was working, his head on his paws.

"Well, Piramus is real fond o' that dog," Leda resumed. "Got 'im trained to do just what 'e wants 'im to. And the dog really loves Piramus, you can see that. But, for all they gets on so well, that there dog 'as to keep 'is place. You'll find that with all of us true Romanis.

"All of us likes the dogs, we does. But none of us will let a dog go inside a wagon or a tent. Whatever you says, a dog is mokardi. That what we was always taught when we was young-uns; mokardi they is, unclean. But, you see, some of these didakai half-breeds today, there's one of 'em I knows, 'e's got a dog 'what 'e lets in and out of 'is vardo just as 'e pleases. Seen it with me own eyes, I did, otherwise I wouldn't never 'ave believed it.

"There was the man sittin' on the ground, and 'e puts out 'is 'and to pat the dog on the 'ead. Well, that was all right, but dordi; what do you think, bor? Well, that dog comes up and 'e licks 'is face; yeah, licked 'im right on 'is mooi 'e did. Nearly made me sick to see 'im. But there, what can you expect from a dirty diddi like that? How about fillin' up your cup again?" Leda interrupted herself to say to me.

She stood up and took the cup from my hand. "Don't have to ask you, do I, me old moosh?" she said to Piramus, taking his cup from the end of the trolley, where he had left it.

She turned back again to me.

"Always a one for drinking a drop of meski, is my Piramus."

And so, the cups were filled and handed round again.

Piramus had finished the red diamonds in his design and was working his way round the trolley with a tin of yellow. He looked up for a moment, as he took his freshly filled cup. He looked at me, jerking his head in the direction of his wife. "We been 'earin' about dogs," he said, "ask her about cats." With an expressionless face, he turned back to his painting.

"Cats!" I said to Leda, "do you like to have a cat about?"

The gypsy woman shook her head vigorously. "Now that's something I can't abide," she told me. "They ain't mokardi like a dog; not unclean like dogs is. Well, they is mokardi, 'cause they licks themselves all over. It ain't that, but, well

there's something about a cat. I don't know.
Course, there's some of our people don't mind
'em, but I can't bear 'em; especially a black cat.
'A black cat,' says the gorgies, 'why, a black cat is
lucky,' they says.

"Funny 'ow they thinks about some things, ain't
it. Now, if you were to ask me, I would say that a
black cat is more likely to be unlucky for you.
See, you never know if a black cat ain't a bun; a
witch, see. I remembers when I was a gal: only a
little rakli I must have been, about nine or ten I
suppose.

"Some travellers stopped just near us, and our
Mam she says to us as 'ow the old woman in
that other wagon is a witch. 'That old woman is
bun,' she say. Well, me and my brothers and
sisters, see, all the lot of us, we took to watching
that old woman – on the quiet, like. There was
the old woman and 'er old man. And d'you
know what, bor?"

Her voice dropped a tone and I almost felt the
hairs on my scalp rising in anticipation of what
she was about to say.

"There was a big black cat there with 'em," she
went on slowly. "The biggest and blackest and

shiniest black cat I've ever seen, before then or since. But this is the most extraordinary thing..."

Leda spoke more slowly now, in a slow, solemn voice.

"The old woman went into 'er wagon, the straightaway that cat came out. Then, after a bit, the cat would go in and the old woman would come out. Once she walked around behind the wagon, then straightaway back came that black cat."

Leda leaned forward a little; her black, fathomless Romani eyes looked straight into mine. Slowly bringing out each word in a tone which almost chilled my blood, she said, "We never seed the old woman and the cat together." Then her words came with a rush: "Because they was one and the same; they was a witch."

After a slight pause, she went on, "There was four of us gals slept together in a tent. That night, when all the others was asleep, I couldn't seem to get to sleep know 'ow. Every time I shut me eyes, I could see that old woman from the vardo down the lane.

"Then, after a bit, I must 'ave dozed off a bit, for I opened my eyes and there was the old woman, a-comin' in through the door of the tent; glided in silent, she did. And I was so trashed, so frightened, that I couldn't cry out; only lie there and look at 'er, was all I could do. First, she bent over Zolias, who was the oldest of our sisters, nearest the door.

"And then she went onto Rachel, who was sleepin' next to our Zolie, in between Zolie and me. And then she started to move towards me. And all the time I was that a-feared I couldn't move as much as a finger. And then, just as she was bendin' over me, some'ow I managed to let out a scream. Well, Zolie, the oldest of us, as was near the door, she woke up at once; then, of course, the other two gals did too.

"And just as Zolie was getting' up, that big black cat went jumpin' out through the door of the tent and disappeared into the night. Course, our mother come runnin' in, to see what it was all about, and she seed that cat runnin' away. So, when I told her all about seeing that old woman in the tent with us, she seen what it was.

"And our Dad got up too, and 'e made the fire up well and we all sat up; never went to bed any more that night, we didn't. Moved off early the next morning and never seed the old witch again. But I never forgot. Oh yes, you can say it was just a child's dream, if you like, bor," Leda said to me, divining my thoughts, "but I knows different."

"No, I don't like cats. But there's one thing I think it's always nice to have," Leda went on. "Always 'ad one when I was a little gal. A jackdaw, I mean. We 'ad one just along the time I was tellin' you about. 'Ad 'im for years, we did. My Dad was real fond of 'im, used to call 'im the kauli rai, just in fun, like (the black gentleman, see), on account of 'im sittin' on the shafts by the end of the wagon and lookin' so perky and thinkin' so much of 'imself. Taught 'im to speak Romani words, our old Dad did. Ain't you never 'eard of a jackdaw talkin', then, sir?"

I countered that I didn't think I had.

"Oh yes, very good talkers they can be. You 'as to take 'em when they is young. Our Dad made a little box for the kauli rai to live in, fixed it on underneath the wagon, 'e did. But 'e was that tame, never 'ad to shut 'im in; used to go in and out of 'is box just when 'e liked, 'e did. And when we was stopped anywhere, 'e'd come out and 'e'd sit on the shaft. Knowed our Dad, 'e did; used to get up on 'is shoulder and then 'e'd walk down 'is arm when we was all sittin' round the fire a-nights. 'E'd come right down and sit on our Dad's 'and. And the words 'e used to say: 'sar shan?' and 'kushti bok'. Wonderful it was to 'ear 'im. 'Ad 'im for years and years, my Dad did."

I must confess that I was beginning to wonder how much longer this story would be! But the gypsy woman continued without hesitation …

"Well, I was quite grown by the time 'e died. A dreadful cold winter, it was. Course the bird had got to be pretty old by then. But 'e got took bad and 'e just lay down and died, part from the cold and part from old age, I expects. But my old Dad was proper upset when 'is kauli rai died. "I won't never 'ave another bird," 'e says, "on account of I've lost me kauli rai. And although we 'ad several different dogs an' ferrets an' that, 'e never 'ad another jackdaw. Even a goat, my Dad 'ad one time; a very good drop of milk she used to give us, though there's some as don't like it. But never another jackdaw, 'e didn't 'ave."

Gypsies have always been horse dealers. Some forty years ago, I used to visit Sturminster Fair, an annual event in May more or less in the middle of Dorset. It's a fair which has existed for centuries, where you are sure to find a few gypsies if you keep your eyes open.

Gypsies love to carry on a conversation in a public place like this, in the pogado jib. And the party that I discovered there one bright and sunny morning was no exception.

A man with a cap at a jaunty angle on his black hair, and a bright yellow and red neckerchief about his throat, was speaking when I first noticed them.

"Kushtiest little groi that tooti ever clapped yocks on", he was saying in a loud voice. "Kek, mandi wouldn't bicken that kushti little groi, not for anything, mandi wouldn't."

There were no more than half a dozen Romani words in this little speech, but they were sufficient to hide the man's meaning from the Gorgios all around. An accurate translation would be: "Best little horse that you ever clapped eyes on. No, I wouldn't sell that nice little horse, not for anything, I wouldn't."

Several passers-by looked curiously at the little party of gypsies but, as might be expected, appeared to make nothing or the words spoken so loudly in the pogado jib. I suppose my unsuspected advantage in being able to follow words only intended for Romani ears, was a somewhat cheap one; but after all, there was nothing really private in what was going on.

The little group of gypsies fascinated me. I recognised this as the opening gambit in a horse deal. Nobody appeared to show any interest. After a pause of nearly a minute, a man with a battered navy blue felt hat with a feather in it remarked that the horse reminded him of one that he'd had a year or two back, "but 'e was that workshy, well I 'ad to sell 'im pretty quick."

The man in the cap flared up at this. To compare his kushti little groi with one that was workshy was clearly offensive. But there was no malice behind the words, and I could see that this was merely preliminary to getting down to the business of transferring a horse from one owner to another.

The gypsies were already arranging themselves into two sides, one of which would support the seller and point out the good features of the animal and the other, which would support the purchaser, and call attention to all its faults.

At first, I took the prospective purchaser to be the man with the feather in his hat. But in this I was wrong, as further developments showed.

An elderly woman, who up to now had taken no part in the conversation, put in a few words. She wore a crimson, patterned headscarf over her greying hair, and a pair of black eyes looked out from a dark face, wrinkled like a walnut. "Wore out, I reckon 'e is," was her contribution.

"Wore out?" the man in the cap replied, heatedly. "Dordi, dordi, I reckon she must be going divio." He looked round the little group of gypsies for support. Half of them laughed loudly, apparently agreeing that the old woman was going divio (mad). The rest reserved a stony silence.

Then a woman who I took to be the wife of the horse-owner turned to her neighbour, a young woman with a baby slung at her hip, and said, "Remember when we come that great big hill in the snow?"

The young woman made no reply. She was on the side of the purchaser, and did not wish to recall the big hill in the snow.

The speaker then turned to her other neighbour, an old, old man displaying an ancient green waistcoat beneath his unbuttoned jacket. He nodded, sagely.

"Yes, I remembers. 'Twas lucky that there 'orse was with us at the time. 'E was only one as we put on siders so as we could take them wagons up that great big 'ill."

The old man was referring to the gypsy custom of applying a "sider" as a means of ascending a difficult hill. The "sider" is a horse that is harnessed alongside the regular horse on a wagon. The first wagon is taken up the hill by this means, and the "sider" is sent back down the hill for the next wagon. This is continued until the whole procession is brought to the top.

The horse which is so used is not necessarily a spare one, but may have its own wagon to pull. It is unharnessed from its own wagon, which is left at the bottom of the hill until last. One of the other horses is then walked back down and harnessed to it, after which it draws it up the hill with the assistance of the "sider".

The old man looked contemptuously around the group of gypsies.

"Yes," he said, slowly nodding his head, "yes, a kusti little groi, that. But then," he went on, raising his voice a little and punctuating his words by tapping on the pavement with a long-handled whip which he held in his hand. "But then, these young-uns nowadays, they don't know a kushti groi when they sees one."

He shook his head sadly. "What things is comin' to today, on the road, well!" He shook his head again, apparently at a loss for words.

The man with a feather in his hat spoke up again.

"Well, 'e looks workshy to me."

The old man looked amazed to think the others should consider the horse workshy and once more slowly shook his head. The old woman immediately opposed him.

"Hark at the old moosh," she said. "Every Romanichal knows well enough the sort of broken-down old 'orses 'e 'as. Where 'e gets 'em from is more than I can tell. 'E ain't the one to be sayin' about 'orses. Well, I mean, what do we know about 'im?"

Then she gave a toothless chuckle, for which purpose she removed the short cigarette from between her lips, after which she swiftly replaced it.

I began to realise that this sort of thing was going to go on for some time!

CHAPTER FOUR –
INSIGHTS AND LEADINGS

As yet, I had not seen the horse that was being discussed. So, it was with considerable interest that I followed the little group when they made their way slowly through the crowd to the rear of the village pub. This seemed to be a sort of gypsy mecca.

Various horses, some harnessed to carts, were being inspected and haggled over. One man was running up and down with a chestnut mare, shouting loudly that this was the finest mare in the fair. The man in the cap walked straight up to a light cart with a chestnut horse harnessed to it. He made an expressive gesture towards the horse and said, "There, kushtiest little groi that mandi ever clapped yocks on!"

This seemed to be where we came in.

But events now took a more practical turn. Almost before I realised what was going on, the old woman had stepped up into the cart, had given a flick to the horse and was off at a cracking pace down the road. Soon the cart reappeared round the bend on its return journey. Its appearance was the signal for cries of encouragement or hoots of derision from the opposing sides in the deal.

I saw now that the old woman was the prospective purchaser and, as she careered round the bend, almost on one wheel, a cloud of dust rising from the hoofs of the chestnut horse, there were shouts of "Go it, old-un, see how that 'orse can run," mingled with "just look, fit for the knackers!"

The old woman drew up with a jerk and, throwing the reins to the man in the cap, jumped down with remarkable nimbleness.

"No, that 'orse of mine would run 'im off 'is legs," she cried. "But, mind you, I'd never part with my kushti little groi. And don't you think I'd ever chop 'im, neither."

I could see that events were now heading for a chop (an exchange of horses), that is dearly loved of gypsies. I began to wonder how long it was going to take to settle the deal, and even if it would be completed that fair day.

Then, without warning, the man with the cap was off down the road at a cracking pace in another cart, drawn by a black horse which I took to be the property of the old woman. Back he came to the accompaniment of more shouts: "Let 'im 'ave 'is 'ead!"

"There now!"

"Did you ever see a horse that could run like tha?"

And "Ho-ho-ho, do you call that a horse? Mind 'e don't drop dead in the shaft's bush."

The man in the cap jumped up and down, and another discussion started. A price was mentioned. "Well, I wouldn't take no less than that."

Immediately there were shouts from the supporters of the purchaser. "Dordi, dordi! Did I hear 'im right? An' fit for the knackers, too."

But the supporters of the seller also had their say. "Is that all he's askin' for that kushti little groi? He must be daft to let it go so cheap."

The man with the feather in his hat appeared to be getting quite excited, and he clapped the owner on the back and said, "You must be crazy expecting to get all that for such a broken-down old animal. Just look at his teeth! Just look how 'is back falls in! He's got a bit of a limp, too. Well, 'e's got a limp comin' on, then. Now, now, tell us 'ow much you really want; really, I mean."

It was surprising to see how the price dropped by rapid stages, to half the original price mentioned. Then arose the question of how much the old woman would take for her horse; and the same procedure was gone through all over again.

Eventually it was agreed that the two should exchange horses. The man was to pay five pounds more than the old woman, but he was to give five bar back. That is to say, the man was to give five pounds back to the woman, to be spent on liquid refreshment at the inn, to see everything neatly rounded off.

What either party gained from the transaction it is difficult to say. But, to the gypsy mind, an hour's entertainment had been extracted from the deal.

The two concerned struck hands on the bargain and all was settled. Striking hands is similar to the gorgio practice of shaking hands on a deal, but instead of clasping hands the gypsy man and woman brought the open palms of their right hands smartly together.

The deal concluded; it was remarkable to see how all the gypsies made a complete change of front. Those who had found fault with the horse now extolled it and congratulated the new owner on the purchase. Each new owner proclaimed loudly that he or she had got the better deal, and everybody was happy.

That night stories would be told around gypsy fires of the day's happenings. Every detail of the bargain, embroidered with a good deal of exaggeration, would be recounted. Each horse would be inspected again, and no doubt proclaimed the kushtiest little groi that mandi ever clapped yocks on.

Of course, this sort of dealing is no more than a side-line; no more than an entertainment, worse than profitless. But many gypsies in past years, when horses were used on farms and in transport, did a steady business in horseflesh. They can be quick and skilled with their hands, too.

Many years ago, the editor of a certain country magazine asked me to write an article on strawberry-growing, illustrated with photographs, showing the whole story from the first planting to the final dispatch of the fruit to various parts of Great Britain.

That was how I found myself visiting various growers, big and small, in the Dorset strawberry country, in search of copy and pictures. I was talking to one of the biggest growers and, as we walked along the long line of plants, among the men and women, the boys and girls, who were busy picking the luscious plants, I asked him, "Do you have gypsy pickers coming and staying on your land nowadays?"

He shook his head.

"Practically a thing of the past for most growers now. But there's a chap down the road, got a smallish holding, always seems a bit behind the times. Most growers have gone over to the climax variety, but he still sticks to the old royal sovereign that used to be popular until a few years back. Go along and see him, why don't you? He always has some gypsy pickers."

I thanked him for his help and made my way out to the road, and drove to the holding he had described.

A handcart, laden with punnets of strawberries, was standing beside the gate. A pretty young girl of, perhaps, seventeen and obviously of gypsy blood advanced towards me with a smile. "Would you like some strawberries, sir?" she greeted me.

I saw no reason for beating about the bush, so I told her the name of the magazine I was working for on this occasion, and asked if I might see the proprietor. She directed me to a gate and, as I walked through it, a tall, elderly man appeared silently from behind a hedge, almost as if he had been waiting for me. He was so obviously a romanichal, with his black, pointed eyes and dark curls, going a little grey, that I found myself greeting him, "Sar shan?"

His old, wrinkled face was inscrutable, as he raised his right hand and replied, "Sar shan?" as though he was quite accustomed to strange Gorgios calling on him every day and greeting him in Romani.

I explained my business to him, and he stood there with his hand on the gate, looking at me with that unmoving, unblinking stare that I have seen so often. "Is it the newspaper that you're from?" he asked me at length, naming a well-known local paper.

Remembering the almost inborn dislike of a man from the paper, I denied this pretty strongly. "Oh no, this is a book with pictures in it that comes out once a month; nothing like a paper at all." I hastened to put the case as well as I could. "You see," I explained, "the editor of this book wants to tell his readers just how strawberries are grown. You know that a lot of people think that all you have to do is to pick the fruit and get a lot of money for it. But really, of course, we know that is not so. You have to work hard all the year round to be able to pick strawberries for about four weeks in the summer. That's what my editor wants to make known to the people who read his book. It's certainly nothing like a newspaper," I wound up.

It seemed I had struck the right note, for the man suddenly smiled.

"You can tell the tale all right," he said at last, with one of those bursts of gypsy frankness, though without the least trace of impoliteness. "Don't mind telling you what you want to know, though it seems you know all about it already."

We talked about strawberries and strawberry-growing for a while. And then I asked him, "Do you employ Romani pickers in your strawberry fields?"

"Never employ anybody but Romani pickers," he answered. "Come on through here, and you can go and talk to them." And so I went, with the old man, to the further end of the field, where some half a dozen women were bent over the crops.

There was one old woman dressed all in black. Her wrinkled face looked all of eighty years and her back, as she stooped over the plants, looked as though it could never more be straightened. But her old, gnarled hands fairly flashed in and out among the leaves, plucking the red fruit and placing it carefully in a basket, which she moved along from time to time as she worked down the row.

The ages of the other women, all obviously of gypsy breeding, must have from, perhaps, twenty to forty-five. "Here's somebody who wants to have a few words with you," said the old man. And, with this brief introduction, he turned and walked back up the field.

The gypsy women did not seem very impressed. Then one middle-aged woman spoke up: "Come over 'ere, sir, and I'll tell your fortune for you; I'm sure you got a lucky face."

"Dordi, dordi!" I replied. "A bokky mooi, tooti pen? Kek, tooti wouldn't want to dukker mandi." This, my best effort, meant, "A lucky face, you say? No, you wouldn't want to tell my fortune." The woman was quite unabashed, and if she was surprised, she didn't show it.

"Oh," she said, brightly, "a rai, eh?"

She went on picking all the time, as indeed did all the other women. I asked her if she had a wagon, and she replied, proudly, "Over there, behind the hedge." I looked where she pointed and could make out the roof and stovepipe of her wagon, almost hidden on the far side of the hedge.

"And haven't you all got wagons?" I asked the other women.

Nobody answered. But the woman who had been doing all the talking answered for them. "No," she said, "all kenniks; house people they are. I'm the only real traveller here." I talked with Menty, as she later told me she was called, slowly keeping pace with the pickers as the moved down the field. At last I made to move off, and was surprised to hear her say, "If you likes to come round our stoppin' place tonight, you knows where we are." I was delighted, even if rather mystified, by her invitation.

"Torarti, then, and kushti bok."

The day deteriorated to a dull, overcast evening and, for a June Dorset evening, none too warm.

The gypsy fire, although burning a bit low, made a cheerful rendezvous. Menty and the old woman in black, that I had seen picking strawberries that afternoon, were seated by the fire. The girl I had seen outside the gate was there, too, and I later discovered that she was Menty's daughter, Zena. Menty's husband,

Neezer, and their son, Evergreen, a boy of about sixteen, completed the party. The old woman, I discovered, was Menty's mother.

She had given up travelling on the death of her husband some six years previously, and liked to sit at the fire in front of her daughter's wagon. She puffed steadily at a short, clay pipe and I had the very clear impression that very little could happen in her vicinity without her knowing all about it. "My old Mam likes to smoke 'er old swegler when she's with us," Menty said. "Smokes fags, like the young-uns does, when she's home in 'er 'ouse."

"Things ain't the same on the road to 'ow they used to be," the old woman grumbled.

She shook her head sadly at her memories.

"When I was a young gal, there wasn't none o' these 'ere motors." She took the pipe from her mouth and pointed the stem at me, to lend emphasis to her words. "I remembers my old Man tellin' us when we was young-uns about two of our family who was took by the police and up before the bisterin' moosh, the magistrate man. And do you know what?"

She replaced the pipe in her mouth and leaned back, so that I could think it over. I shook my head. "Well," she went on, "they was sent to Orstralier; nobody never seen 'em no more."

It took me a while to realise that she was referring to the old convict settlement in Australia. "Botany Bay," I murmured, in realisation.

"Ah, that's it," said the old woman, "Botany Bay! Fancy you knowin' all about it, sir."

This little episode seemed to put me up in her estimation. So friendly did she become that she was soon telling me her pet grievance, which, Menty told me afterwards, was something she would only do to somebody she took a fancy to.

And so the old woman took a fancy to me.

"Now see here now, sir," she said, leaning towards me a little. "I reckons I must be about eighty-five or six, or maybe eighty-seven." She paused and regarded me through the smoky haze rising from the fire. She spoke quietly and almost without expression and yet, when she paused, the effect was dramatic. Of course, centuries of fortune-telling and playing on the credulity of countless gorgio women through many ages, has bred a race of gypsy women who know instinctively when to raise the voice, when to let it fall, when to speak quickly, when to speak slowly, and many other simple but highly effective tricks of elocution.

So, the old woman paused dramatically, and I waited.

At last she took her short, black pipe from her mouth and pointed the stem at me. "Yes, I'm all that old. Stands to reason, don't it." She was sure she was well over eighty. "Yet there is them that gets old age pension," she said bitterly, "and they ain't nowhere near as old as me."

"See, she ain't got the gorgio papers to say she was born," explained Menty. "It seems that if you 'ave the gorgio papers to say you been born, you gets a pension when you're old. But the old woman ain't got none, see, and they don't count it else."

We talked to each other and told each other of the injustice being done to the old woman, who had become a kennik, a house-dweller, and embraced the gorgio ways, only to be told that she could not draw the gorgio pension.

Presently, Evergreen fetched some wood and threw it on the fire. The kettle was boiled, and cups of tea were handed round. At last, I stood up to depart, and then my invitation became clear.

"Oh, before you goes," said Menty, as though she had just thought of something, "before you goes away, we've got a letter from our other boy, Manfo. Doin' 'is national service, 'e is. Perhaps you'd like to read it for us, would you?"

Naturally, I replied that I would be delighted to be of such service. I sat myself down again, more tea was poured out, and all the company sat still and silent. The letter, already opened, and of limp and much-handled appearance, was postmarked several days before. But whether or not it had been read already I had no means of telling, though I think not. It was quite an ordinary letter from a young national serviceman to his parents.

I could imagine the young gypsy in his irksome army kit, having of necessity to bow down to tiresome regulations, while some army lad, a gorgio friend who had mastered the difficult craft of letters, wrote the string of symbols on a piece of paper, so that Manfo's words could be heard by the fire of his parents, many travelling days distant in rural Dorset.

Gypsies are quite indifferent to the gorgio ways of reading and writing. I remembered a time when a man I had come to know quite well had his wagon pulled in behind a "Trespassers will be prosecuted" board. "I reckon them words on that bit o' board says I don't 'ave to stop 'ere," he told me, "but I can't read 'em, so I don't know that!"

The Romani system of trail signs, known as the patrin, is all that is required. A broken piece of stick, an uprooted tuft of grass, a small sliver of bark, cut and left hanging, a tiny piece of rag in a hedge, all can have a message for a party travelling behind. And, moreover, are secret from the gorgio eyes of gavers and veshengros, policemen and gamekeepers.

Family histories are handed down by word of mouth, through the generations. This is women's business. Among them a few entertaining and fanciful tales, like the story told by Homey Smith ...

Homey folded her hands loosely in her lap, as she sat on the lowest step of her wagon and in a low voice she began, "A long, long time ago there was a great king. And this great king, he ordered for to be built for 'im a great palace. Everything was to be the bestest that could be 'ad and the men that was to build it were to be the cleverest that could be found. And it took a very long time to build 'cause it was so big, and because it 'ad to be so good, but at last came the day when it was finished. And the great king, 'e called together all the men that 'ad worked to build it for him, so that there could be a great hawing and peeving (a great eating and drinking).

"Soon they all comes to this great feast. And there was much food, all on gold plates, and much strong drink, all in gold cups. And they all sat and ate for a long time. And when they was all full up, so as they couldn't eat or drink any more, all the men that were there started arguing, who was the bestest one among 'em.

"First up spoke the man what 'ad drawed up the plans and told 'em the right shape of all the different parts. 'Without me,' 'e says, 'there couldn't 'ave been no palace. Then up spoke the man that 'ad laid the bricks and built all the walls. 'Without me,' 'e says, 'there wouldn't 'ave been no palace.' And then up spoke the carpenter. 'Without me,' 'e says, 'there wouldn't 'ave been no doors and no furniture. Without all those things, there couldn't 'ave been no palace.' Then up spoke the man what 'ad put all the glass in the windows. 'I fixed glass in a thousand windows. Without me the wind and the rain would 'ave blown in. Without me,' 'e says, 'there couldn't 'ave been no palace.'

"And after that, they all stands up, one by one, and tells of the different things what they all done; and each says there couldn't 'ave been no palace if it hadn't 'ave been for 'im. And all the time, the great king, 'e just sits and 'e don't say nothing, only 'e listens very careful to 'em all. Then, at last, they suddenly spies a dark man, standing apart from all the others, just inside the door. 'Come inside and tell us who you might be,' says the great king. So the dark man steps right inside the great hall. 'I am the smith,' 'e says, in a loud voice, so that all could hear 'im.

"Then they sees 'ow 'is face is all black from the forge and he's still got his leather apron on, where he's come straight from his work. Then one or two of 'em there, them that was all dressed up in fine clothes, looks down at the smith and start sayin' to one another, 'What right 'as that man in 'ere, 'e ain't done nothin' towards buildin' this great palace for the great king."

"So, at last, the great king, 'e turns to the smith an' 'e says, 'Now, answer. What right 'ave you in 'ere? Can you say as 'ow you done anything towards building this great palace?' And the smith, 'e smiled and 'e speaks up and 'e says, 'We've heard the window-maker, we've heard the carpenter, we've heard the bricklayer and all the other men that reckons to be the most importantest men of all. But I says that not one of 'em could 'ave anything without their tools. An' who was it that made their tools?' And the man stopped and looked all round while they thought about it. Then he speaks up again. 'Yes, none of 'em could 'ave done anything without their tools. And who made their tools? Why, it was me, the petulengro, the smith. And now,' 'e says, drawin' 'imself up, for 'e was a tall man, 'now I'll ask the great king to tell us who he thinks is the most importantest man of all.'

"So then the great king, he stands up and 'e says, 'You've all heard what the smith says. And it is a great truth that not one of you could have done any work at all without the tools that the smith made. Therefore,' 'e says, 'I say as 'ow the smith is the most importantest man of all.' And then the great king, he has a place made for the petulengro by his right hand, and the smith sits down, all in 'is working clothes, with 'is apron on and 'is face all black from the forge. And the great king, 'e give 'im food to eat and drink in a gold cup, with 'is own hand."

Homey paused to lean back a little.

"And that smith that I've been telling you about, 'e was the first petulengo, the very first smith that started all our family long ago."

It was a good story, and Homey told it so well there in the warm, orange firelight that it seemed to be quite true.

CHAPTER FIVE -
ACCEPTANCE AND TRUST

Over the years various filmmakers have made films claiming to portray gypsy weddings. Elaborately dressed actors ebb and flow through intricate routines, violinists feverishly play, and a young couple are at the centre of an elaborate ceremony. I have no doubt that the gypsy desire to oblige, and give the customer what he thinks he wants, as well as an eye to bringing personal financial benefit to himself, has contributed largely to this. In fact, most Romani weddings are quite simple affairs, like the joining of hands before an assembly of members of both families.

Often the two families consist, in the main, of the same people, for marriage between first

85

cousins is looked upon favourably. An elder, in a leading role, will be in charge. Sometimes, a little loaf of bread is broken into two pieces, a thumb of each marriage partner is pricked, and a drop of blood is made to fall on a piece of bread. Then the two pieces are exchanged and eaten.

In the past, the couple sometimes jumped the broomstick, which meant joining hands and then stepping over a branch of the wild broom, which had to be in flower at the time; the flower signifying a fruitful marriage, with many children. I've been told that this was of tinker origin and not Romani. The variation carried out by tinkers was called jumping the budget (the budget being the box in which tools of the trade were kept).

The tinkers are another nomadic race, distinct from Romanis, and they, too, have their own secret language called shelta. In later years, when a gypsy couple are said to have jumped the broomstick, it means no more than a simple elopement. There is nothing casual about this. Once a couple have gone off together, there is no going back, although after a short interval they must return to the bride's family for the groom to make his peace with them.

Now, many weddings take place in gorgio fashion, in church or registry office. The acquisition of gorgio papers, recording the event, is seen as something useful to obtain. In the past, gypsy men sometimes had two wives; usually, though not always, two sisters. And the two intertwined families seem to have got along without encountering any particular difficulties.

The gypsy living wagon developed during the second half of the nineteenth century. Who was first with the new invention we may never know, but the new, superior way of living spread fast among former tent-dwellers. It was preceded by the two-wheeled pot-cart that could have its shafts run into a hedge or a bush to ensure that its floor remained level when the horse was out of the shafts. Cramped though it must have been, sleeping on the board floor must have been luxury compared to sleeping on the damp earth.

Coverings that had previously been used to improvise a tent would be spread over cart and occupants, a relatively snug arrangement. Slightly bigger four-wheeled pot-carts followed, some with a light wooden framework to support a canvas tilt, but they were devoid of all interior fittings that became standard for living-wagons which came later.

There are several different types of vardo, all of which could be seen in years gone by on the back roads and lanes of Purbeck – and in fact in many other places in our beautiful county - but they are all to a standard interior layout. The footboard, behind the shafts, is in front of the door, which is divided horizontally, half-way up, like a stable door. As you enter, there is a tall, narrow cupboard from floor to ceiling, on your left.

Next beyond it is the stove, with airing cupboard above, extending to the ceiling; the stovepipe within it is double skinned, so that clothes can be warmed with no risk of scorching. The stove is always on the off side of the vehicle, where the stovepipe is least likely to suffer damage from overhanging tree branches, as the vardo travels narrow country roads.

Behind the door on your right, as you enter, is the china cupboard, its glass front at forty-five degrees, making a triangular shape to fit the corner.

Further along on the right, opposite the stove, is a locker, which serves as a seat and as storage space. The woodrus (the bed) is across the back end of the wagon. Usually, it has curtains to shut it off during the daytime, and it folds or slides into a single bed width but can be drawn out to form a double bed. Outside, across the back end is the cratch, a kind of sturdy rack, on which a miscellany of articles, ranging from kettle irons to tent coverings, can be carried.

More often than not a bundle of herbs, considered unlucky if brought inside the vardo, is tied to the axle. Underneath the rear end is the pan box, which contains the big, black pots and other culinary equipment.

There is always great pride of ownership in the vardo, for it is by far the most valuable possession the gypsy has. In the early years of the twentieth century a first-class wagon could cost twice as much as a small house. It is a mark of the owner's importance and financial standing. There were many firms of coach and carriage builders who could undertake building whatever vehicle a purchaser desired.

Every vehicle was a one-off job. Mass production was, as yet, unknown. But it was not long before specialist builders began to emerge, like Dufton's, who built a particular type of vardo, later copied by other builders. The body was of matchboard construction, with outside ribs, all ornamentally carved, the sides leaning outwards as the rose from floor to ceiling. Being outside the body, the large rear wheels had to be set wide apart, but this made for good stability. The swivelling front wheels were of much smaller diameter.

The deeply arched roof carried a lantern, sometimes called a mollycroft, along its centre, and there were also windows at its sides and at the rear. The ledge wagon also had large-diameter rear wheels, but they were accommodated differently and on a narrower track. The side walls rose from the floor between the wheels, but above the wheels they were stepped outwards forming the ledge. The body was of matchboard, with carved outside ribs, like the Reading Wagon. Side and rear windows were fitted, and some ledge wagons had a mollycroft roof.

Large-diameter wheels, although cumbersome, were more easily managed on rough or soft ground. The Burton Wagon had all its wheels small enough to be accommodated beneath the body, so that the floor-width was not restricted by their track. The parallel sides stood perpendicular to the floor.

One or, on some wagons, two side windows were fitted, as well as a mollycroft roof. The bow-top wagon, sometimes called the barrel-top, was of much lighter construction. A framework of bent wood, usually ash, each rib in the form of an almost complete circle, was covered in canvas and the interior lined with cloth. Roof and sides being curved, it could not be fitted with windows and the only possible place for them was the matchboard rear, and that was of little practical use for the little curtain across the bed shielded its light from most of the interior. All four wheels were beneath the body, the front swivelling ones usually a little smaller than the rear ones.

The square bow-top sounds like a contradiction in terms, but it was a very satisfactory development of the bow-top. Its construction was similar, but the bent wood formers were flattened at the top and over the sides, so that a section of the wagon body could be said to be square with rounded corners. The flat sides made it possible to fit windows, overcoming the bow-top's big disadvantage; lack of light.

The type that appeared in some numbers soon after the end of the last war was the open lot, though a few seem to have been made in the 1930s. The open lot can be professionally made, but most are home-made DIY jobs, starting with a flat cart. Usually a wooden framework is built on the cart and a tarpaulin covering spread over it. The front is open, with a movable canvas curtain hung from the top of the opening. Other methods of building vary with the builder's ingenuity and the suitability of materials.

I knew one family I used to meet from time to time just south of Dorchester, on the road to Upwey. They had an open lot made mainly from plywood obtained from tea-chests. Though lacking a little in symmetry, it was sound enough and served the family for many years. Some owners of elaborate, professionally built vardos looked down on the humble open lot, calling them peg-knife wagons, suggesting that their simple crudity was the result of them having been fashioned from the same knife that made the pegs, as the only tool. But those were only the simplest of the type. Some open lots were quite smart vehicles, even having some carving and several colours of paint.

In the early years of the twentieth century that new invention, the motorcar, made an occasional appearance. There being no suitable Romani word that could be applied to the horseless carriage, a name had to be invented; and the gypsy word meaning motorcar became 'hummer'.

Now you may think that name was chosen because of the sound a car engine makes. Not so.

Early motorcars did not hum. They clanked, they rattled – rhythmically, maybe - but the slow-revving engines of those days did not hum. A friend of Romani descent, who knows about these things, told me how it came about. A man who had just bought a brand-new car showed it to a gypsy man whom he knew. Seeing a car for the first time, the gypsy asked, "What's it called?"

The proud owner, thinking he was being asked to name the make of the car, replied, "It's a Humber." So, with the gypsy way of omitting the odd consonant here and there, every car irrespective of make became, in gypsy parlance, not a Humber, but a hummer.

There is one more type of living-wagon worthy of mention, representing as it does a transition from horse-drawn vardo to motorised version. They are very rare and, as far as I can recall, I have seen only one example. It consisted of a lorry with a plain, flay deck, with the body of a vardo (a ledge wagon, I think it was), shorn of its wheels and undercarriage, standing upon it. There is a name for such hybrids – they are called 'whoopies', a name also applied to gorgio-style caravans, drawn by a car or lorry.

Gypsy crafts and occupations were mainly based on natural materials, free for the taking. Basket-making, gathering and selling wildflowers, like daffodils, broom-making, making artificial flowers from wood and paper, all are traditional gypsy occupations. Also of gypsy manufacture were those little picturesque dome-shaped beehives made from straw, and seen now only in pictures.

Important to most gypsies was horse-dealing. When horses became so few and far between, some gypsies became house-dwelling kenniks and took up the used car business. With their versatile adaptability, they learned how to coax a little more life from elderly vehicles of doubtful performance. Tatting, the collection of rags, bones, and scrap metal, has always been a gypsy occupation too.

But most well-known of all must be clothes-peg making. My old friends Piramus and Leda showed me the whole process.

Piramus sat with his legs slightly apart, stretched out in front of him. Between them he had driven into the ground a straight piece of birch, about three inches in diameter. This little post, which protruded about a foot from the ground, he called the stale. By his side was a pile of rods, each about three feet long. Piramus held his knife in his left hand, supporting it with his knee, and drew a stick back and forth along it, turning it with each stroke, so that the bark was rapidly and evenly skinned off. In a remarkably short space of time, he had skinned a whole bundle of sticks.

The next job was to cut them into clothes-peg lengths. This is where he used the stale, the little post he set up between his legs. He took a stick and, at an appropriate distance from one end, rested it on the stale with the knife blade on it. Then, with the aid of a piece of wood in his right hand, used as a mallet, he drove the knife into the stick and severed it.

Leaving the piece where it had fallen, he moved the stick along and cut another piece and so on, until he had only an odd piece left at the end. He threw this into the fire, took another stick and carried on as before. I admired the easy accuracy of his work, for there could not have been as much as a quarter of an inch difference in length between the longest and the shortest piece. I have been told that gypsies use a piece of stick as a gauge, concealed in the hand, but if Piramus used such a gauge I could not see it. His only comment was, "Easy when you're used to it."

'Tinning them up' came next, and consisted of encircling each peg with a narrow strip of tin, secured with a tack.

While Piramus had been cutting the wood lengths, Leda had been busy pulling the bottoms off several old tins with a pair of pincers. Then she cut them up beside the seam, so that the metal could be flattened.

Next, she cleaned each sheet, rubbing with earth to remove the paint, then polishing it with moss until it shone. Finally, she cut the tin sheets into strips with scissors. With the whole pile tinned up, Piramus started to go through them again, making a split in each peg. To do this quickly needs a sure hand and an equally sure eye, for the split must be made exactly half-way down the wood.

The inevitable pot of tea was made, and cups handed round. But the two energetic gypsies spent hardly any time at all over their tea.

Leda sat herself down beside her husband, with a substantial-looking knife in her hand. Taking a peg in her left hand, she swiftly made two cuts to chamfer the wood on the inside where the pegs would be slipped over the line.

"Puttin' a mouth on 'em, that's what we calls it," Leda told me. "Tain't 'ardly worthwhile makin' 'em, not really," she went on, as the pegs fell one by one from her quick hands onto the heap. "A few miles I shall have to walk, carryin' all this lot. Don't sell 'em all that easy. All the gorgio women seems to have all the pegs they wants.

Course, there it is, all us people makes 'em that good they last for years and years, don't never wear out. 'Ave to go into town with 'em. The 'ouses is closer together in towns; don't 'ave to walk so far and you can make more calls much quicker."

I visited Heavenly Bottom again a few years ago, when I made a programme on location for BBC Radio Four. The grassy valley floor is still there, but it is a recreation ground now, fronted by a row of bungalows. The itinerant musician of gypsy appearance, whom I say there, with his antique accordion, was a link stretching back over seventy years to when I knew Heavenly Bottom in the heyday of gypsydom. A quiet air of mystery seemed to hang over that place of such nostalgia. Maybe the mullahs, the spirits, of long-departed Romanichals still linger there.

Whatever may be, I'm glad to have shared with you just some of my memories of those strange and wonderful people who used to roam the byways of Old Dorset.

Kushti bok.

APPENDIX - GLOSSARY

There now follows a unique glossary of Romani words compiled by G.E.C. Webb as a result of his numerous meetings with them. This is a fascinating and valuable resource. As the language was essentially a spoken one and not a written one, there is no set spelling.

Adray – there
Akai – here
Apray – on, above, over
Arva – yes
Atch – to make camp, to stop
Atching Tan – camping place
Atoot – across
Atrashed – afraid, frightened
Avree – away

Bar – pound note

Bavol – the wind
Bender – round-topped tent
Besh – sit
Bibi – aunt
Bicken – sell
Bister – a summons
Bisterin' Moosh – magistrate (literally summonsing man)
Bitcherin' Moosh – ditto
Bok – luck
Bokky – lucky
Boler – wheel
Boobi – pea
Boodega – shop
Bor – friend
Bor – hedge
Bori – big
Bori Lon Panni – the sea, the ocean
Bosh – violin, fiddle
Boshmengro – violinist, fiddler
Bun – witch (slang)

Chai – woman (used, I believe, only for a Romani woman)
Chavi – child (more correctly, girl child with chavo meaning boy)
Chin – to cut
Chiriklo – bird
Chop – to exchange
Chor – to steal
Chovihani – witch

Churi – knife
Corona – crown

Dadrus – father
Dai – mother
Del – give
Didakai – half-breed gypsy
Diddi – shortened version of didakai
Dik – see, look
Dikker Glim – looking glass, mirror
Diklo – handkerchief
Dinelo – silly
Divio – crazy
Divvus – day
Dordi! – well! (usually said twice – dordi! – well I never!)
Drabengro – doctor (literally poison man)
Drom – road
Dui – two
Dukkeriben – fortune telling
Dukkerin' – shortened version of dukkeriben
Dunnik – cow (slang)
Dykers – daffodils (slang)

Feeta – clothes peg (slang)
Folki – folk (used only, I believe, for gypsy people)

Gad – shirt
Gav – town
Gaver – policeman

Giv – farm
Givengro – farmer
Gooi – pudding
Gorgie – corruption of gorgio
Gorgio – non gypsy
Groi – horse
Groiengro – horse dealer
Guddle – to catch fish with the bare hands

Haw – eat
Hobben – food
Hotchi – shortened version of hotchiwitchi
Hotchiwitchi – hedgehog

Jaul – go, travel
Jib – speech, language
Jin – to understand, know
Jivaben – life
Jukal – dog
Juke – short for jukal (dog)
Juval – woman

Kairengro – one who lives in a house
Kako – uncle
Kavvi – kettle
Kavvi Saster – kettle iron
Kauli – black, dark
Keddin' – picking
Kek – no
Kekkeno Moosh – nobody
Kenner – house

Kennik – one who lives in a house (alternative to kairengro)

Kettin' – another form of keddin', meaning picking

Kitchema – public house, inn

Kor – fight

Kosh – stick

Kova – thing

Kushti – good

Lav – word

Lel – take

Levinor – beer

Levinor Mengris – hops (literally beer things)

Lil – book

Loli – red

Loli Berries – strawberries (literally red berries)

Lon – salt

Looger – catapult

Luller – to take

Mandi – I or me

Matchi – fish

Matchko – cat

Meski – tea (contracted form of piameskri)

Mokardi – unclean

Mooi – face (or mouth)

Mooi Kosh – whistle pipe (literally mouth stick)

Moosh – man

Mort – woman (not a Romani)

Muller – die (also the spirit of a dead person, ghost)
Mullerdi Poove – churchyard, cemetery
Mumper – tramp, low class van dweller not of Romani blood
Mumpli – like tramps

Nafli – ill, unwell
Nappi – workshy (when speaking of a horse unwilling to work)
Narkri – bad, evil (not Romani)

Otchemengri – frying pan

Pal – brother (shortened for of pral)
Panni – water
Panni Gurni – frog
Peeve – to drink
Pen – sister
Pen – speak, say
Petulengro – blacksmith (also the Romani surname of the gypsy tribe of Smith)
Piameskri - tea
Pirri – foot
Pobbo – apple
Pobbo Keddin' – apple picking
Pogado – broken (often corrupted to poggered)
Pogado Jib – broken language (meaning a mixture of Romani and English)
Pooker – speech, the Romani tongue
Pookerin' Kosh – signpost

Pooro – old
Posh – half
Posh Corona – half crown (old fashioned coin)
Posh Rat – half breed gypsy (literally half-blood)
Pootsi – pocket
Poove – ground, earth, field
Poovengro – potato
Poover – shortened version of poovengro
Porni – white
Pral – brother
Praster – run

Rai – gentleman (pronounced "roy")
Rakli – girl
Raklo – boy
Ran – the ridge pole of a gypsy tent
Rarti – evening, night
Rat – blood
Rauni – lady
Rocker – to speak, to talk
Rom – man, husband (only refers to a Romani)
Romanes – the name of the Romani language
Romani – gypsy
Romanichals – gypsies (literally Romani men, with romanichais being gypsy women)
Ruckers – trees
Ruckersamengri – squirrel (literally tree creature)
Rummer – marry
Russlers – flowers

Sar Shan? – how are you?
Saster – iron
Scroops – hops (slang)
Sherri – head
Shoshi – rabbit
Solivardo – light cart
Stale – the short post on ewhich a peg maker works
Stiraben – prison
Swegler – pipe

Tan – camping place (also used for tent)
Tatchi Tatcho – true, real
Tatchipen – truth
Tatting – rag and bone dealing
Tompad – parson (slang)
Tooli – beneath, under
Toot (or Tooti) – you
Toove – to smoke
Toovalo – tobacco
Torarti – tonight
Trashed – frightened, afraid
Trin – three

Vardo – living wagon
Veshengro – gamekeeper (literally woodsman)

Wast – hand
Welgora – horse fair
Weshengro – gamekeeper (another form of veshengro)

'Witchi – hedgehog (short for hotchiwitchi)
Wonger – money (literally coal)
Woodrus – bed
Wooster – thro

Yock – eye
Yog – fire
Yogengri – firearm, gun
Yogger – corruption of yogengri
Yorya – egg

ALSO BY G.E.C. WEBB

G.E.C. Webb's classic novel depicting Dorset life in a forgotten age, "Sinfi's Secret – a Gypsy Family Saga" is available as eBook and paperback.

Enter a world long gone as you read the moving story of the life, loves, and loss of a true Romani as could only be told by beloved Dorset author G.E.C. Webb. This emotional journey is based on the fascinating and unique personal experience of the author who was a student of the mysterious Romani race and its secret language, and was one of the few 'Gorgios' to be accepted by them to sit beside their fires.

The story opens long ago in the heyday of Gypsydom, with a family proud of its pure Romani blood, its gaudily painted caravans, and skewbald and piebald horses. But all is not well.

A crude carving of a bird is viewed with superstitious fear. One of the sons commits the unthinkable sin of marrying the daughter of a house-dweller.

Tragedy follows, and Auntie Sinfi of the Second Sight foretells the end of the Romani race.

Unbelievable as it seems, cold dread is felt by all. For isn't Auntie Sinfi always right?

This gripping story with its authentic insights into the Romani way of life, although fiction, has the authentic air of a documentary. Travel with the Dorset gypsies on an emotional journey through World War, general strikes, and jazz in the roaring twenties. Lean times in the thirties lead on to another World War and even more and faster change. Only one thing does not change. The ancient feud with the Jelcutt clan. Can this ever be resolved, and will a true Romani ever find happiness with a Gorgio girl, away from the campfires and the road?

Printed in Poland
by Amazon Fulfillment
Poland Sp. z o.o., Wrocław